The Princess Marries the Page

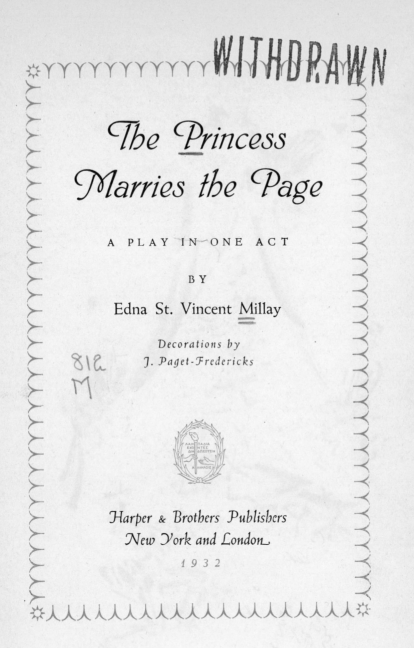

The Princess Marries the Page

A PLAY IN ONE ACT

BY

Edna St. Vincent Millay

Decorations by
J. Paget-Fredericks

Harper & Brothers Publishers
New York and London
1932

To Edith Wynne Matthison

Note

The Princess Marries the Page has had four productions, of which the following programs give the details of time, place, and casts:

Vassar College

Poughkeepsie, New York

May 12, 1917

The Princess   *Edna St. Vincent Millay*

The Page   *Ellen D. Gailor*

The King   *Josephine Palmer*

The Lord High Chancellor   *Ellen L. Hoffman*

First Soldier   *Katharine Shepard*

Second Soldier   *Persis Holden*

Third Soldier   *Joyce Buchanan*

The Bennett School

Millbrook, New York

October 22, 1917

The Princess   *Elaine Orr*

The Page   *Margaret Gage*

The King   *Sara Verity*

The Lord High Chancellor   *Roslyn Morey*

First Soldier   *Marion McDonald*

Second Soldier   *Dorothy Reed*

Third Soldier   *Josephine Parrott*

*Produced by Charles Rann Kennedy
and Edith Wynne Matthison*

❧

The Provincetown Playhouse

New York City

November 22, 1918

The Princess   *Edna St. Vincent Millay*

The Page   *Vadim Ureneff*

The King   *Hutchinson Collins*

The Lord High Chancellor   *O. K. Liveright*

First Soldier   *Robert Edwards*

(viii)

Second Soldier   Louis B. Ell

Third Soldier   Frederick Ward Roege

Directed by the Author

Scene by C. M. Sax

❧

Cosmopolitan Club

Philadelphia

December 22, 1930

The Princess   Mary Kennedy

The Page   Guido Nadzo

The King   Dudley Digges

The Lord High Chancellor   Wright Kramer

First Soldier   Samuel Barbour

Second Soldier   Alfred Richards

Third Soldier   Gian Carlo Minotti

Setting by C. Grant La Farge with the co-operation of

Mrs. Houston De Coursey

Original music by Deems Taylor

Staged by Mr Digges

Costumes by courtesy of the Metropolitan Opera Company,

Helen Arthur and Helene Pons Studios

❧

(ix)

Preface

The Princess Marries the Page was written when I was an undergraduate at Vassar College, that is to say, it was finished then; I had begun it several years before. It is my earliest attempt at play-writing, one of my earliest literary efforts in any direction, and but for an accident would have been published some thirteen years ago. The accident to which I refer was my losing of the manuscript.

There were very likely several copies of the manuscript in existence at the moment when I discovered that I had mislaid my own. The play had been performed by the students at Vassar, and by the alumnae of the Bennett School at Millbrook; later it had been produced by the Provincetown Players in New York; quite possibly some of the actors still held copies of it. And even had all the copies been destroyed I could doubtless have rewritten the whole thing from memory. But just at this time I was very busy writing and arranging a group of poems which—after having

(xi)

borne successively the tentative titles of "A Stalk of Fennel"; "Poems"; and "City Trees"—were to appear under the title "Second April". And everything else seemed of relatively small importance to me. I made no effort to find or to reconstruct the lost play.

Some time ago, when searching among my papers for something which in thirteen years I shall very possibly find, I came upon the manuscript of *The Princess Marries the Page*. Miss Mary Kennedy and Mr. Deems Taylor were my guests at Steepletop at this time, and it happened that Miss Kennedy was looking for a one-act play to be produced by the Cosmopolitan Club of Philadelphia. I brought forward as a doubtful possibility my recovered manuscript. To my astonishment and pleasure it proved to be just the sort of thing required.

On reading over to myself *The Princess Marries the Page*, I found that I liked it much better than I had expected to do. It was unmistakably a youthful work, and very slight, but I thought it rather pretty. And I had a desire to see it among my published books.

So here it is.

E. St. V. M.

Paris
June 1932

The Princess Marries the Page

The Princess Marries the Page

SCENE

[*A room in the top of a tower. Half the room is to be seen, bounded by a grey wall which curves away from the audience. In the centre of the wall is a large open window, framed by reddening ivy and flooded with sunlight. On the outer ledge of the window, in the sunshine, sits a slim and handsome Page, playing on a pipe. Inside the room, in a very big chair, reading a very big book, sits the most beautiful Princess you have ever seen.*]

PRINCESS

I came up here to read! . . . Go down!
Play in the court—there is a fountain there;
Or in the garden, where are coloured roses;
Go to the cook, who's making cakes today,
And say I said you were to have your fill;

(1)

Only, disturb me not; I came up here
To read.

    I came up here to play.
Go down! Read in the garden—where are wasps,
Or in the court—where there are coloured lizards;
Go to the King, who's making search today,
And say that I have climbed unto a ledge
Of air, and play a pipe, and will not come;
Only, disturb me not—I came up here
To play.
[*Plays*]
    Tu-luri-lu! Tu-luri-la!

PRINCESS

This is my father's tower—you just go down now!
I have to read this reading, and I can't
Read while you play—you ought to know I cannot!
Besides, you throw a shadow on the book.

PAGE

I have to play this tune; 'tis in my head
And clamours to be out! Who knows? It may be
The last that I shall play!—there is a thought
Should comfort you.
[*Plays*]

(2)

Original music composed by Deems Taylor and played by the Page in the production at the Cosmopolitan Club, Philadelphia, in 1930. The above facsimile, and that on the following page, are reproduced from manuscript supplied through the courtesy of the composer

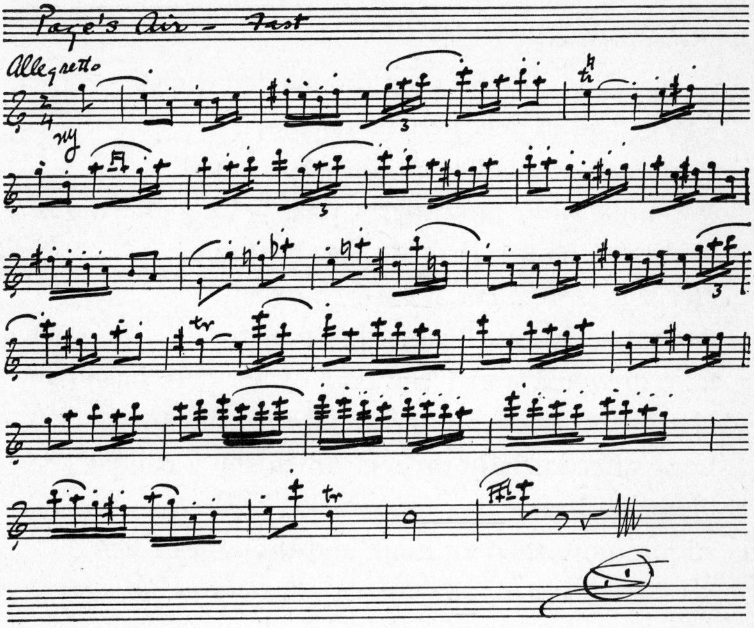
Page's Air – Fast
Allegretto
mf
tr
tr
tr

[*Reading aloud*]

    "So then the maiden came
Clothed all in delicate colours, like a garden,
And very sweet to smell; her little hands
Were like white moths i' the dusk,—long afterwards
In dreams he saw their drowsy fluttering—;
Her soft, infrequent phrases, hurriedly
Articulate against his lips, her eyes,
Like drowned stars i' the pool of her dark hair;
Her breath upon his neck,—all these he knew,
Long afterwards, in dreams; when she was gone
He stood beside the honeysuckle bush
Alone, more than an hour, and thought of her."
[*The Page, who has been playing a sad and lovely melody,
  has gradually ceased playing, charmed by the Prin-
  cess' story; in the same way the Princess, enraptured
  by the Page's piping, has been reading more and
  more slowly, softly, and abstractedly, until she has
  ceased altogether. They now turn to each other simultaneously.*]

Don't stop!

PAGE

That's beautiful!

(3)

PRINCESS

Go on!

PAGE

Go on!

[*They gaze at one another for a moment, then the Page laughs amusedly. The Princess turns from him in anger.*]

PRINCESS

I hate you!

PAGE

By my soul I do not blame you!
A piper that will dumb his pipe with myrtle,
And pipe no more;—almost I hate myself.

PRINCESS

I would I had the grace my fathers wore,
So I might pry you off the ledge, or tear
The ivy from beneath you, that you might
Find your way down without it!

PAGE

And I would
Your hair were longer,—I would seize you by it,
And my grey ladder not descend alone.

(4)

PRINCESS

My hair is very long! It is too long!
It is too heavy! It weighs down my head!
Oh, how I hate you! How I hate you! Oh!
[*There is a sound of some one coming up the stairs.*]
Hark! Is that some one coming here?—I'll wager
A hawk against a tennis-ball my father
Wants you and comes in search of you! Climb down
A little way, and cling to the ivy! Quick!
[*The Page climbs out of sight below the window, the Princess goes back to her book.*]
[*Enter the Lord High Chancellor.*]

CHANCELLOR

I crave Your Highness' grace for this intrusion.

PRINCESS

I know your errand, sir.

CHANCELLOR

      Madam, you know it?

PRINCESS

Aye, sir, my father—

CHANCELLOR

      Madam, the King, your father—

(5)

PRINCESS

Has tried to feed my goldfish once again,
And Blue-Fin will not eat! You tell him
Blue-Fin does not like oat-cakes! And besides
He dropped his crown i' the bowl one day, and
    scared them!
Tell him I say to leave my fish alone!

CHANCELLOR
[*Very solemnly*]
Madam, it is not fish.

PRINCESS

Oh, never tell me
He has found my journal! Oh, he has not the right
To read my journal, e'en though he be a King!
Snatch it away!

CHANCELLOR

Madam, your royal father
Sends me to ask if you perchance have seen
A wretched page, in russet hose and doublet,
About the tower; 'tis said he turned this way.

PRINCESS

A page. A page? H'm, let me see, page—page—
There's been no page i' the tower—that I can swear to;

(6)

Indeed, I've sat here all the afternoon,
And not a soul, until yourself made entrance,
Has come into this room. Nor have I heard—
Assure 'm of this—a single sound below me;
I have not heard one step upon the stairs.
Page—page—huh-uh!
[*The Chancellor starts to go; as the Princess begins to speak
again, he turns and listens. She is leaning against
the window, speaking loud enough to be heard by the
Page.*]
                I know the man you mean!
A piping fellow, and discourteous,
New to the court, I know! You'll come upon him
Asleep somewhere i' the sun, mayhap, or else
Flat on his back beneath a hawthorn-bush,
Love-piping to some freckled shepherdess!
As for the tower—nay, sir, he is not in it.

CHANCELLOR

I thank Your Highness, Madam, and crave grace
For this intrusion.

PRINCESS

            Nay, sir, I am glad
If I have been of ne'er so slight assistance
To one in need.

[*Curtseys*]

My reverence to the King.

[*Exit the Chancellor.*]

[*With amusement*]

"There's been no page i' the tower—you'll come
   upon him
Asleep somewhere i' the sun, mayhap"—mayhap
You will, and then again mayhap you will not!
Mayhap most anything! How do I know
But he has fallen asleep, or found a tree
To flute beneath—mayhap if I could see
Through a wall—to make no mention of the ivy!—
I then might tell what's going on without;
As 'tis—troth's me! I know not!

[*The Page leaps into the room.*]

Shrive my soul!

Who told you to come in?

PAGE

Madam—his pages
Are passing by beneath in search of me!
I sue for pardon—in a moment more
They will be gone. I would ha'e gi'en me up
Rather than plague you further, only that
I feared if they should take me on the wall

[*He goes on bravely, but with embarrassment, not looking at her*]

(8)

'Twould spread a tale that you had hid me here
For love, and lied to cover my escape.

PRINCESS

For love? For love of you? Lied—out of love
For you? Heav'n's blessing on me! Do I look
As if I loved you?

PAGE

[Distressed]
Nay, I said not so,
Your Highness—

PRINCESS

Do I look as I would lie
To shield you from a beating?

PAGE

[With emotion]
Nay, indeed,
I do not think so! Since in all the world
Is not one tongue so fond would lie to shield me
From death.

PRINCESS

[After a pause]
Why, boy! Why, nay, then, you are wrong;

(9)

For that would I. In all the world not one?
What of your sweetheart? Is there not some maiden,
Some golden-headed herder of white geese,
Some shepherdess, some dark-eyed violet-vendor
That holds you dear? Some fisher-girl, that daily,
Swinging her basket, barefoot, crosses the court
And turns to smile at you?

PAGE

Madam, there is not.

PRINCESS

[*Aside*]

'Tis difficult to explain: where are their eyes?
I' faith, he is not ill to look upon!
Clothed like a gentleman, myself should find
Him perilous,—aye, and even as he stands,
I' faith, he is not ill to look upon!
[*To the Page*]
Where is your mother?

PAGE

An it please Your Highness,
I think she be in Heaven, with your own.

PRINCESS

Have you no father?

(10)

PAGE

Aye, I have a father,
Such as he is.

PRINCESS

Poor boy,—in all the world
Not one! Come here!
[*She holds out her arms to him. As he starts forward toward*
her she drops her arms with shame and some confusion]
There is a bit of cobweb
Caught in your hair. So!
[*She removes the cobweb, an imaginary speck, from his hair,*
then kisses him suddenly on the cheek, and turns away,
appalled at herself]
Prithee to forgive me!
[*She begins to weep*]
I could not bear to see thee so distressed,
And no one caring!

PAGE

[*Deeply stirred*]
Lady, do not weep!
I am no longer sad, save for your grieving.
Melt not my tears for you, that for myself
Lie like a frozen pool i' the breast,—I pray you,
Weep not, sweet soul,—I am not worth your tears.

(11)

PRINCESS

Nay, that may be;—there's many a worthless thing
Wept over!
[*Turns to him in instant deprecation of her rudeness, and takes
      him into her confidence, her voice rising into sobs and
      finally coming out into a wail at the end of her speech*]
                  I am not quite sure for what
I do weep; but I have not wept in days,—
And it is time I did—now that I'm at it—
I might as well keep on—and weep it ou-u-ut . . .

PAGE

[*Deeply distressed and entirely at a loss*]
Please do not cry so! Listen, wouldn't you like
My silver pipe to play on?

PRINCESS

[*Still weeping*]
                  No—no, thank you!

PAGE

[*Hastily searching the big pocket-bag he wears at his side*]
I have a golden string long as a lance.

PRINCESS

I have a golden train longer than that.
[*Sobs*]

(12)

I have a peacock's feather.

PRINCESS
[Unpleasantly, looking up]
Aye, no doubt!
Plucked from the tail of my most favourite fowl!
You may retain it.
[Crosses away from him]

PAGE
[Uncertainly]
Well, I have—I have, then—
[Finds an apple in his pocket]
Do you like apples?

PRINCESS
[Very eager]
Apples? What about them?

PAGE
Why—do you like them?

PRINCESS
[Humiliated but desirous]
No! That is—no, no!
At least—

(13)

[*She turns and surrenders to him with an appreciative smile*]
Have you an apple?
[*Sees it*]

Give it to me!

PAGE

[*Holding it out of her reach*]
Ah, but so easily won? And such an apple?
So ruddy and incomparable a fruit?
[*He looks quietly into her face, which is very near him, and
speaks playfully but intensely*]
What have you in your pockets for exchange?

PRINCESS

[*She is held by his gaze for a full moment, then drops her eyes*]
Pockets? Exchange?
[*She looks at him, but again drops her eyes*]
Nay, I have nothing, then.
[*She remembers the apple*]
Oh, but please give it to me—please!—I love
Apples!
[*Suddenly becoming very sweet and imperious*]
I want it so, I have to have it!
[*The Page, amused, after a slight pause gives it to her*]

PAGE

Against such reasoning is no debate.

(14)

[She seizes the apple and scurries with it to the seat in the window, where she begins to eat it, with both hands, like a squirrel. He goes up to her little throne and sits insolently in her chair, one leg over the arm of it]

PRINCESS
[With a deep sigh of satisfaction]

Ah-h-h!

[Looking up and catching his amused and almost paternal smile, she holds out her hand to him with an instant access of tremendous, but mock, dignity]

You may kiss my hand.

[The Page drops to his knees before her, and seizing her hand in both his, bows his head over it. He does not move for some time, and the Princess becomes very uneasy. She wriggles her hand a bit to free it; but he does not release it. She looks about the room nervously, and then back at him; she scowls, and wriggles her hand again. Then she laughs in a bit of terror. Finally she has a thought, and proffers him her apple]

[Very hospitably]

Bite?

[The Page looks up at her, and seizes her other hand, apple and all. His face is tragically sad]

What's the matter? Why, you look so sad!

(15)

And so I am . . . the saddest man, mayhap,
That e'er your eyes beheld.

PRINCESS

[*Deeply touched by his grief, but considering*]
                              The saddest man
I ever saw? Ah, no—that cannot be!
For I have looked upon that wretched King
Who rules the wide dominions to the west—
The "Sullen King" men call him—but I know
That he is only sad; he was so sad
The day I saw him, that I needs must pat
His cloak to comfort him! At least they say so;
I have forgotten,—I was very small.

[*The Page has risen at the mention of the Sullen King, and
    turned from her; at the close of her speech, however,
    he comes back, and stands looking down at the top of
    her head, which she has hung in pretty embarrassment,
    like a child*]

PAGE

It is a sovereign remedy, this patting
Of gentlemen's cloaks by ladies,—be they small
Or not so small;—I would I wore a cloak.

(16)

PRINCESS

[*Very brightly, grateful that they are playing once more*]

Yet, surely in your pocket still remains
Some certain cure for sorrow! Let me look!

[*She makes room for him on the window ledge; he jumps up
    beside her*]

Give all you have, and I will choose among them!
Oh, what is that?

PAGE

That is a stripèd stone
To keep away the fairies.

PRINCESS

[*Examining it*]

But who wants
To keep away the fairies?

PAGE

[*After a delighted pause*]

Well, I have, then,
A fluted shell to conjure them about.

PRINCESS

[*Reaching for it greedily*]

Give it to me!

(17)

Ah, but I need it more!
You've but to call them, and they all will come;
Whilst I—ah, many's the night I've waited for them,
Thirsting, and fasting, and adrip with dew,
I' the depths of some dark bosk—until they should
Appear and dance about me in the clearing;
But never once beheld them, never once
Even so much as caught the fragile clangour,
Incredibly, of their clear bugles and bells,
And high, sweet, rollicking shouts—until I found
This.

PRINCESS
[Awed]
And they come now?

PAGE
Aye, on any night
When the moon is white and the woods are black, and scarves
Of silver mist are drawn, and then withdrawn
About the trunks of the trees—ah,
[Closes his eyes]

aye, they come.
[They have both been looking ahead of them with wide eyes,

(18)

as if seeing the same thing, while the Page has been
speaking. When the Page sighs "Ah," and closes his
eyes, the Princess echoes the sigh, and closes her eyes,
too. At the close of the speech, however, she suddenly
becomes very alert, and leans toward him beseechingly]

PRINCESS

Oh, sometime take me with you! I have never
Beheld a fairy!—Oh, I *say* I have,
Because I *may* have.
[*Considering, with a frown*]
              And it seems I *must* have,
So that I'm *sure* I *have*—but all the while
[*Rapidly, and in a lower voice*]
Down in my heart I know I *never* have.
You understand.

PAGE

[*Elaborately*]
           Aye—or at least, that is,
I may, so that it seems to me I must,
And I am sure I do—though all the while
Down in my heart of hearts, I am convinced
I do not understand you. Women are
Superior to men in every way,
But chiefly in the intellect.

(19)

PRINCESS

[*Joyfully*]

'Tis so!

And so I will protest until I prove it
To all who doubt.

[*Aside, to the Page, comically*]

Albeit I know 'tis false.

[*They both laugh. She takes another bite of her apple, and comes back to the treasures scattered on the window ledge*]

Well, is that all you have? There's little here
To balm a wound.

PAGE

[*Stuffing the things back into his pocket*]

Aye, it is all I have.

PRINCESS

Nay, but I heard a crackling under your hand!
What may that be? Out with it! Give it to me!

PAGE

[*He has leapt from the window, at her words, and crossed away from her*]

No, no! Oh, no, no, no! You must not ask me!
It is—

[*He does not continue, but turns his face from her*]

(20)

PRINCESS

It is a letter from a girl,
That's what it is!

PAGE

Well, then, what if it is?

PRINCESS

[*Mortified, extravagantly protestant*]
Why, nothing! Why—why, nothing! Less than
    nothing
To me! What do I care about your letters?
You speak as if you thought perhaps I cared,
Was jealous, maybe, of your paltry letters!
Why, what is it to me, who writes you letters?
Or how many letters she writes? I'm only glad
It's not *my* letters that you bear about
To flaunt before my face—I mean, her face—
I mean I'm glad I am indifferent to you,
And wish that you had died e'er ever we met!

PAGE

Lady, be comforted, for I shall die
Full soon. But as for this, it is my grief
Itself, and should be pleasant to your touch.
[*He gives her the paper which he had in his pocket. It is
    heavily official-looking, and bears a large seal*]

(21)

Ah, for a little while I had forgotten,
But now I do recall. Lady, I thank you
For this sweet play.
[*He looks at her with intense tenderness, then turns abruptly,
and goes to the window*]
                    The sun is off the ivy
Now, and the darling world is growing dark.
[*He turns to her and speaks very gently, as to a child*]
Tonight I think the fairies will come forth.
Here: you may have my shell if you would go
Tonight and watch them dance,—for it may be
They could not hear you calling, through their clatter.
Be there at moonrise.

PRINCESS

[*Fearfully, not taking the proffered shell*]
                    Aye, but where will you be?

PAGE

[*As if struck by the thought for the first time*]
Where shall I be? But where shall I be? Why,
'Tis strange to think upon.—I do not know
Where I shall be.

PRINCESS

[*After a terrified pause*]
                    What is this dreadful paper?

(22)

It frightens me! Oh, I am terrified!
[*Drops the paper on the floor*]
What is the matter?—Tell me! Everything
Is strange about you and the things you say!
Ah, what is that!
[*She gives a little nervous scream and goes to the window*]
[*After a slight pause, reassuring herself*]
                    Nay, it is nothing. Nay!
There's some one on the bridge!
[*Stiffening with horror, she turns slowly, and looks at the
        Page*]
                            It is the guard!
Is't you they seek?
[*Rapidly, but pitifully, without assurance*]
                    A heavier punishment
Belike, for this long absence?

PAGE
                    Nay, indeed,
A heavier punishment,—the heaviest
Of all; but not for absence,—rather for
My presence at the court. I am a spy,
Madam, and map your father's ruin!—My father,
Such as he is!—is king unto your borders.

PRINCESS
Oh, no, no, no! You are not! No, you are not!

(23)

Dear child! Oh, my heart, you lovely, lovely child!
[*He starts toward the door*]

PRINCESS

Where are you going?

PAGE

Down to meet them.

PRINCESS

Ah,

No, no! And yet—oh, this is terrible!
I came up here to read! Why did you come here?
I was so happy till you—

PAGE

Why did I come here?
Why does a man who is doomed to Hell for ever
Climb into Heaven for a day? I came up here
To look into your lovely, angry eyes!
To listen to your sweet, inclement voice!
I came up here to laugh! I came up here
To play!
[*He lifts the pipe to his lips*]

PRINCESS
[*Reaching out for it*]

Oh, no! They are in the tower! The window!
It is your only chance!

PAGE

[*Wearily*]
Nay, I am weary
Of chances. Grant me the grace to bide with you
Until they come.
[*He lifts the pipe again*]

PRINCESS

[*In anguish*]
Oh, don't! Out of the window!
[*With sudden exasperation*]
'Twill save your silly life! Do as I bid you,
Fellow!
[*Remembering his rank*]
Oh, sir, if they take you in this room
'Twill spread a tale that I have held you here
For love—will it not please you to be gone?

PAGE

I am your servant ever, and God forbid
That they should say you loved me!—As for my life,
'Tis but of small account without your love.
[*He bows very low, and lowers himself out of sight beneath*]

(25)

the window. The Princess picks up the paper. Going
back to her chair, she thrusts the paper into her book,
and searches feverishly for something suitable for read-
ing aloud when the soldiers shall come in. Finding noth-
ing, she begins to extemporize, speaking in a high voice
to represent the lady, and then in a very low voice to
show the knight]

PRINCESS

[Pretending to read aloud]

Whereat the youth replied, "Madam, my life
Is but of small account without your love.
Say if you love me." "Nay," replied the lady,
"But rather hate—or would hate if I could;
And since I cannot, do so all the more!
Art satisfied?" "Nay, then," replied the youth,
"That am I not, nor see I any logic
In what you say."

[To the Soldiers, who have entered some time since, and whom
she has pretended not to see before]

Shrive me! Good afternoon!
Chains and mischances! Now what have I done?

FIRST SOLDIER

We crave Your Highness' grace, we thought we heard
Two voices in the tower.

(26)

PRINCESS

[*As if delighted*]

Nay, not really?
Two voices! Nay, but hear me then again!
Where was I—Oh! "Look not in me for logic,
Nor in no lady," quo' she, "nor on oaks
For quinces—you'll not find them—fare you well."
"Madam," replied the youth, "Madam, b'r Lady,
And by my halidome, and by my troth,
And by my knightly spurs—" "Oath me no oaths,"
Quo' she. . . . Nay, is it not well done?—Two voices!

FIRST SOLDIER

The book is upside down.

PRINCESS

[*After a slight pause, brightly*]

Aye, and why not?
That is the way 'tis written. Look and see.
[*She holds out the book to them in turn, so that they see it,
    upside down*]

FIRST SOLDIER

'Tis so.

SECOND SOLDIER

Aye, so it is.

(27)

THIRD SOLDIER

Why, so it is.

FIRST SOLDIER

It is a foreign book.

SECOND SOLDIER

Aye, true.

THIRD SOLDIER

'Tis so.

FIRST SOLDIER

I crave Your Highness' grace. This fellow here
Vowed that he heard two voices in the tower.
And so I thought—

SECOND SOLDIER

Nay, then, not I—I said—
I *thought* I heard two voices!

FIRST SOLDIER

Then 'twas you!

THIRD SOLDIER

Nay, sir, not I! Indeed it was not I!
I only said it *sounded* like two voices—
And so it did.

(28)

FIRST SOLDIER

Aye, that it did.

SECOND SOLDIER

It did that.

FIRST SOLDIER

Your Highness, pardon us.

PRINCESS

With all my heart,
Good sirs—it was a natural mistake.
[*The Princess takes up her book again, and begins to read.
The Soldiers go toward the exit, and there meet the
King and Chancellor, who are just entering. The Sol-
diers fall back against the wall as the King enters
the room. The Princess does not know what has
occurred*]

KING

My dear, I came to ask you—

PRINCESS

[*Jumping up, startled, in such a way that her book falls to
the floor, and the paper falls out of it*]
Why, Papa!
[*Curtseys hurriedly, and speaks very rapidly, without in-
flection*]

Your-Majesty's-health-and-may-Your-Majesty
For-ever-reign. . . . Papa! What do you mean,
Climbing about the tower with a foot
Like yours? . . . When will you learn to be discreet?
Your crown's on crooked—Father, is that your best
   crown
You're wearing every day? Oh, dear! Here! . . . There!
[*She straightens his crown*]

KING

My dear, I came to ask you, have you seen—

PRINCESS

Now, Father, have I seen! What should I see,
Shut up in a tower and bending over a book
All afternoon? What could I see? Instruct me!
And now you're here—answer without evasion!
You're so evasive, sometimes!—Have you been
Experimenting with my goldfish, Father? . . . Father!
You have, you know you have!

KING

           My dear, I came—

PRINCESS

Quite right—to make confession of your fault!
But I shall not forgive you. . . . I have spoiled you,

(30)

Forgiving you so often—and this time,
I assure you, I am grievously annoyed!
Henceforth you will be spared the ignominy
Of losing to me hopelessly at chess
Five evenings in the week. . . . In solitude
I'll walk abroad, and take my goldfish with me
Wherever I go.

KING

[*Troubled*]
        My dear, I beg that you
Will reconsider this so rash decision.
Think of my loneliness, I beg of you.
[*Slowly*]
Five evenings in the week.

PRINCESS

        Well, I will think.

KING

Moreover, you exaggerate, and grossly,
To say I constantly am beaten by you
At chess! 'Tis at the best a matter of chance,
Even if it were the case, which I will not
Admit it to be,—and as the matter stands,
I say that you exaggerate!

PRINCESS

[*With intensity*]
Natheless
I'll wager I can weary you ere dinner!

KING

Accomplished!—Now! My sack four times a day,
Openly, and no comments, Miss, against—
That necklace that you covet.

PRINCESS

Oh, I grieve
To think how long you will sit thirsty, Father,
And blink before my jade magnificence!

KING

That is as shall be seen. Out with you now!
Yet stay—it seems to me—I have forgotten—
Precisely what it was—and yet it seems
To me, I have forgotten—

PRINCESS

[*With pretended lightness*]
You will remember
Later, belike.

KING

Belike, —and yet—it seems—

(32)

CHANCELLOR

Your Majesty, if I may make so bold,
You were about to—

PRINCESS

[*Hastily*]

Very true. You were
About to—lose to me at chess! Oh, Father,
Come along, will you?

[*She is dragging him with her toward the door, when the
Chancellor spies her book on the floor, and goes to get
it for her*]

CHANCELLOR

Highness, Your Highness' book.

PRINCESS

[*Seizing it*]

I thank you.

[*She looks feverishly through it for the paper. The Chancellor
picks up the paper from the floor, and is about to give
it to her when the King, made suspicious by her anxiety,
intercepts it, and takes it*]

Oh, I thank you!

[*About to take it*]

KING

[*Taking it and motioning her away*]

(33)

                              What is this,
My dear?

                    PRINCESS
            It is a private matter, Father,
It is—it is a testament of love
To me, and not intended for your eyes!
[*Trying to snatch it*]
I beg you to return it, sir!

                      KING
                    Soft! Soft!
[*Examining the document*]
I can believe it was not meant for me,
And will return it later; but your lover,
Having had the inadvertence to adorn his prayers
With sketches of the drawbridge and the moat
And one fine silver-point o' the secret passage
Under the chapel,
[*Turning to her*]
                    small wonder if I do
Remember now the thing I had forgot!
Madam, give heed: we seek a fugitive
From the court, a thankless boy, lately our page
And playmate, now our enemy, the son
And spying servant of our sullen neighbour;

His life, when he is found, answers his crime.
'Tis said he turned this way. Now, have you seen him?

PRINCESS

In sooth, how should I know if I have or have not
Seen him? Doubloons! Is he the only page i' the court?
How goes he clad?—I saw a scarlet page,
Fair, and immoderate fat—so that I laughed,
[*Laughing*]
A-fishing in the moat, if it is he
You seek—oh, the fat fellow!—let him escape!

KING

The man goes not in scarlet that we seek.
Thou knowest the scarlet page is a fond fellow
Born at the court, and for his father's sake
Retained. Where didst thou come upon—?
[*Points to the paper*]

PRINCESS

[*With exaggerated protest. She is gradually losing her steady
nerve, and is becoming peevish and hysterical*]
                                    "Thou knowest!
Thou knowest!" sayst thou! Is it a gentle thing
To say, "thou knowest"? "Knowest thou not?" were
    gentler.

(35)

[*Flaring up and turning upon him with reproachful accusation*]
When well *thou* knowest how easily I forget
Who passes in and out, and toward, and thence,
And up, and down, and round about, and over!
"Thou knowest!"

KING

[*Angrily*]
　　　　And so thou dost, and I'll be bound so!
Whence comes this paper?

PRINCESS

[*Subsiding*]
　　　　　　　Sir—it was on the floor—
And I thrust it in my book—the ribbon is lost
That marked the place—I had not looked within it,
Nor knew what it contained.

KING

　　　　　　　"A testament
Of love," I think you said.

CHANCELLOR

　　　　　　Your Majesty,
If I may make so bold—

(36)

PRINCESS

[*Furiously*]

Aye, but you may not!
So bold is too bold, sir! I do not like you!
Be silent in my presence!

KING

And thou in mine

Be silent!
[*With repressed wrath, very rapidly*]
I wish to know if you have seen—
Or, failing that, if you have heard, touched, tasted,
A russet page, or got the scent of him
On any wind—and if so, in what quarter!
[*The Princess, who has been told to be silent, stands like a silly
child, pressing her lips together, her finger on them*]
Well, well, can you not speak?

PRINCESS

[*With mock humility*]

Aye, sir, when bidden—
"If I may make so bold—"
[*Suddenly losing her temper altogether*]
I came up here
To read. "Page—page—page—page"—! I have nei-
ther smelled

Nor tasted your page!
[*More softly*]

And if I had seen or heard
Or—
[*Slowly*]

touched him with my hand—I should remember.
[*Loudly again*]
There is no spy i' the tower—unless he be—
[*To the Chancellor*]
Among *your* retinue!

KING

Enough of this!
I sought straightforward speech, and you evade me
At every turn. "There is no spy i' the tower"?
Is there a page?

PRINCESS

[*Thoroughly frightened, and now thoroughly confused*]
No, sir, there is no page *in* the—
I mean to say—there is no *page* in the—

KING

[*Tripping her at once*]

"No page *in*
The tower"! So! 'Tis a game!—and we shall find him
Under the tower, perchance, or on it?

(38)

PRINCESS

[*Wearily*]

Nay,

I beg of you, I will no longer jest,
But answer straight. I know the man you mean:
A stranger, different from the rest—who goes
In russet, playing on a silver pipe.
Father, unless it is the truth I say,
May dogs run out and bark at me, and children
Flee from me in the street! May my warm body
Be buried in lime, and my soul sit in Hell!
I swear to you, by my dead mother's tears,
And by my hope
[*Staring straight ahead of her*]

to look on her in Heaven,

I have not—

PAGE

[*Who has for a moment been listening from the window ledge,
expecting to be delivered up, now, understanding what
she is doing, and horrified at her terrible perjury and
consequent damnation, leaping into the room*]

Lied—to shelter such a man!

[*Turning to the King. He does not once look at the Princess*]

Your Majesty, in terror of your chase
I climbed into this tower and begged for hiding;

(39)

Whereat Her Highness, out of her sweet pity,
But knowing not my sin, lodged me without.

PRINCESS

Oh, think what you have done! Now they will take
   you
And shut you in a cellar, with mouldy walls—
And rats—and standing water—and tomorrow—
If you survive the night—you will be hanged!
I care not for my soul—I never knew it!
It is a stranger lodging in my house!
I care not when it leaves! But as for you,
I'd set my heart upon your being saved.—
[*Weeping*]
I think you might have let me.

KING

[*Watching her*]

Sir, my daughter

Seems to be fond of you.

PAGE

Your Majesty,

It is but pity, it will soon be spent.

PRINCESS

[*Making up her mind to her course of action*]

(40)

Nay then, it is not pity, and I care not
Who calls it what it is. Do as you will,
Father—I will not live without this man.

Your Highness—!

Silence, fellow! Father—

Nay,

I will not have my life so purchasèd!—
When well I know—

When well you know! In sooth,
What know you—save to scramble walls, and blow
Indifferently along a silver stick?
Be silent whilst I speak, that am informed
Upon this matter! Father, from the hour
Wherein yon
[*Turning to Page*]

scurvy mountebank sees death,
Shall you sit childless.

[*Distressed*]

(41)

But, my dear—my dear—

PRINCESS

I know what you would say: "Affairs of court
Cannot be so conducted, that the man
Is after all a spy, and as a spy
Convicted, and so punishable—
[*She delivers this in a singsong, perfunctory court-room voice*]
                              All of which
Is true.
[*Turning to the Page*]
                    And *more* is true! But this as well
Is true, sir—that I may not live without him.
[*After a tense moment, during which no one has spoken, she
          turns furiously on the Page*]
Be silent!

PAGE

          Nay, I said no word, Your Highness.
[*Softly*]
I had no word to say.

KING

                    By my crown and sceptre,
A difficult affair, and one requiring
Most delicate government.

(42)

[*To Soldiers*]

Await without.

[*To the Chancellor, who thinks to remain*]

You, too.

[*Exeunt Chancellor and Soldiers*]

Now, sir, you may defend yourself.
If your defence shall merit your release,
I will not hold you further. You may speak.

PAGE

I offer no defence, Your Majesty.

KING

So? 'Tis a bitter thing for you to be
Defenceless now—have you no word to say?

PAGE

[*Gently*]

None, sir. I am sorry.

KING

Well—

PRINCESS

Remember, Father,

What I said!

(43)

KING

[*Anguished*]

My child!

PAGE

[*To Princess*]
Your Highness!

PRINCESS

Oh, be still!
Think you you are the only living thing
May die tomorrow? If I set my hour
At the same stroke with yours—what is't to you?
None goes so lonely to his death but thousands
Pass through the door with him. Be not offended;
I shall not crowd your grave. Nor need you feel
'Tis that I loved you!—'Tis but that when you
Are dead, I shall be amorous of death.

PAGE

[*After a long pause, speaking with difficulty, as if the words
were very hard to pronounce*]
Your Majesty, there is upon my person,
Thrust through the inner lining of the doublet,
Above the breast—a—letter, that I would
Your men might take from me.

(44)

KING

What ho! Without!

[*To the Soldiers, who enter*]
Make search upon this gentleman, and take
From him, with courteous fingers, what he hath
Concealèd on his breast—i' the inner doublet.

FIRST SOLDIER

Aye, sire.
[*Goes to the Page and takes a paper, which he gives to the
King*]

KING

Your pardon, sir, that I read it forth.
[*Reads*]
"Undutiful and disobedient sir,
My son, that for a woman's hair and hands
And arbitrary favour, have abandoned
My side, to bear aloft the tail of a gown,
And serve sweet suppers, kneeling,—once again,
And not again hereafter, I command you:
Deliver up your lord into my power.
Upon that chart which heretofore I sent you,
A map I long have cherished, you will find,
By a scarlet rood made manifest, a door
Leading from out the chapel crypt into

(45)

A long and narrow passage underground;
On Saturday, which is the seventeenth,
At twilight, when the King and all his court
Are at their common prayers i' the chapel slumbering,
Do you await my men at the end of the passage
And open to them. Not again hereafter
Shall I command you thus. Fulfil me now
Herein, or from my living presence be
For ever banished." The seventeenth
Is when?

CHANCELLOR
[*Consulting tablets*]
Your Majesty, the seventeenth
Was yesterday.

KING
[*To Page*]
Sir, your defence is more
Than adequate, being noble. You are free.
But ere you go, somewhat I have to tell you:
Your father—

PAGE
[*Who has turned and gone to the window at the beginning of
the letter, now coming swiftly to the King and kneeling, with great emotion*]

(46)

Oh, gracious Majesty, forgive him!
He is an old, old man. No harm can come
To you through him—there is the only paper
[*Pointing to the chart.*]
He held that might betray you: he but sits
And broods all day—it is a sickness with him.
He is too sad, sir, since my mother died:
He hates me for her death, and hates all men
Because they live—and all men hate my father!
I pity him—his life is one big hate
Ingrowing on itself! Oh, sire, bear with him
A little while! He will not live long!

KING

[*Very gently*]
                                    Boy,
You have outlived your father by a day.

PAGE

[*Rising slowly*]
Nay—is it so?—Oh, sir, I would that I
Had been beside him in the final hour!
They say that oft in death a gracious softness
Comes over the most hard—and the old days
Return to them!—I would that I had been there!

(47)

KING

[*Very gently, pausing*]
My boy, you are a King.

PAGE

[*Without interest*]
                    Aye, so I am—
Oh, sir, I would with all my heart, that I
Had been beside my father when he died!

KING

Girl, when thy father, who hath been to thee
Gentler than some, 'twould seem, bows him in state
For the last coronation, see that thou
As nobly mourn. Sir, I would call thee Son,
But that the name might grieve thee.
[*With assumed playfulness and lightness, pointing to the*
    Princess, who turns her back to him as though repudiat-
    ing his suggestion]
                              When thou hast
Accomplishèd thy quarrel with my daughter,
Come in to dinner! And yet—ah, yes, I am told
That lovers never eat!
[*To the Chancellor*]
                    Attend us hence!

(48)

[*To the Soldiers*]
Conduct me to my chamber!
[*Exeunt the King, Chancellor, and Soldiers*]
[*The Princess has gone back to her chair, and is pretending
    to read from the book; but she is humming, to show her
    indifference. Unfortunately, she is humming the very
    tune the Page has played from time to time, during
    the action of the play. Finally her humming dwindles
    into a half sob, and she looks up at the Page, who is
    standing beside her*]

PRINCESS

I am sorry
About your father—I am very sorry—
[*In sudden panic*]
Go—go eat your dinner!

PAGE

[*Boyishly*]
I am not hungry!

PRINCESS

[*Quite simply*]

Neither

Am I.
[*Simultaneously they remember the King's words, and laugh.*

(49)

The Page comes close to her, and would take her in his arms, but she shrinks from him]
No, no! Sweet cousin-prince! Majesty!
I do beseech you!
[*After a moment of silence, during which neither stirs, the Princess turns to him and stretches out her hand. He drops to his knees and presses his lips to it*]
When didst thou love me first?

PAGE

[*Gazing at her*]
When first I did behold thee!
[*Still playfully looking into her eyes*]

PRINCESS

Aye, to be sure.
But when was that?

PAGE

[*Gravely*]
'Twas once upon a time.
You came into my father's council room
And stood beside his chair, and needs must pat
His cloak to—
[*Dropping his head on her knee*]
comfort him!

(50)

[*Looking up almost instantly, and speaking in a tone of worshipful indulgence, as to a very small child*]

"At least they say so—
You have forgotten—you were very small."

PRINCESS

My love, my love! Can love endure so long?

PAGE

Longer than life!

PRINCESS

And we shall live alway!
[*Looking down at the book*]
I came up here to read!

PAGE

Aye, so you did!
I fear me you have lost the place, sweetheart!

PRINCESS

Belike—but then, it does not greatly matter;
The more I think on it, the more I feel
I've read the book before, or if not that,
[*Laying her cheek to his*]
That I have somewhere heard the end of the story!
[*They are both looking out straight ahead of them as—*]

The Curtain Falls

Set by hand in Weiss Antiqua Type
by Arthur and Edna Rushmore
at the Golden Hind Press
Madison New Jersey
Mcmxxxii